HAPPY HALLOWEEN

COLORING BOOK

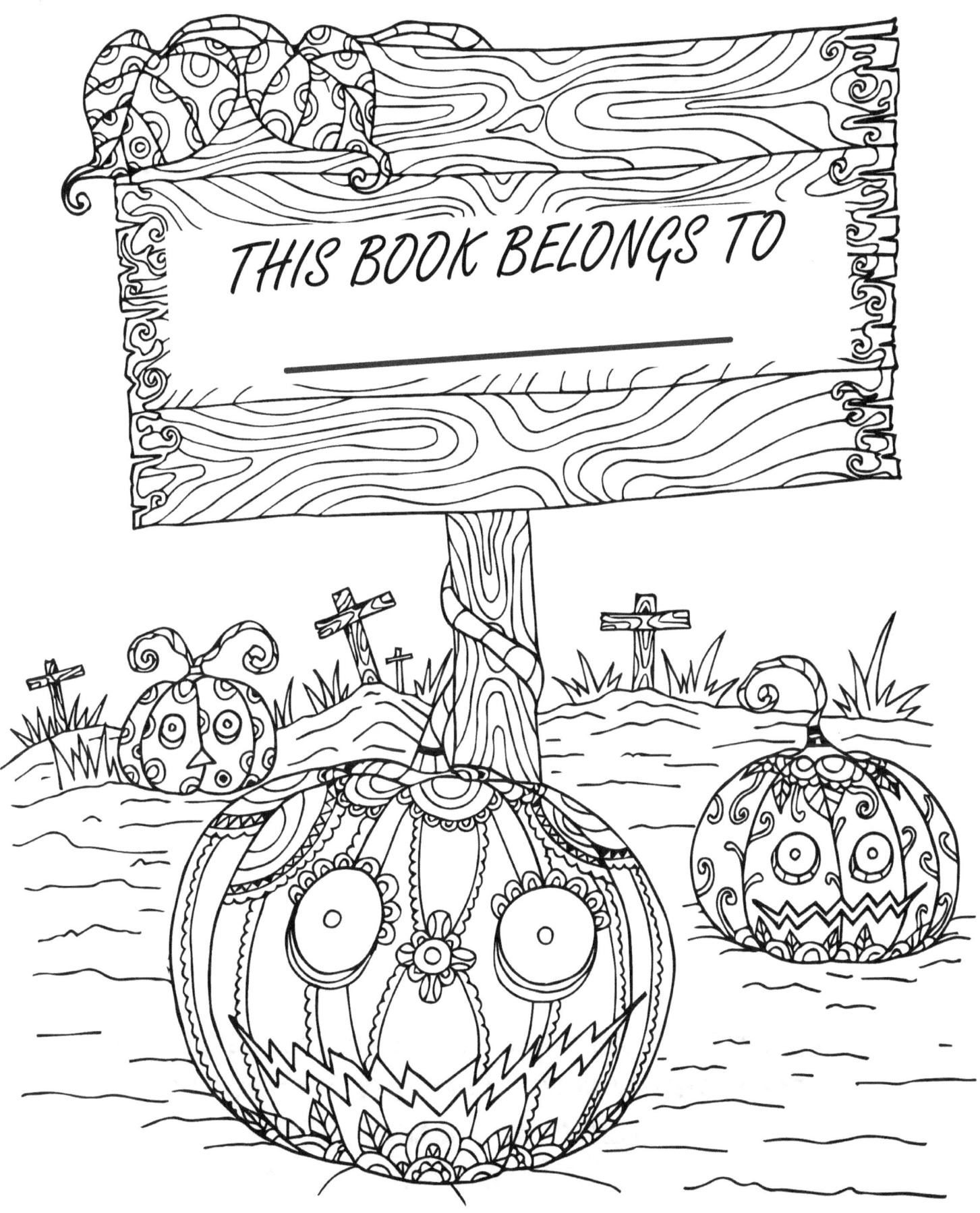

""Halloween wraps fear in innocence, as though it were a slightly sour sweet. Let terror, then, Be turned into a treat..."

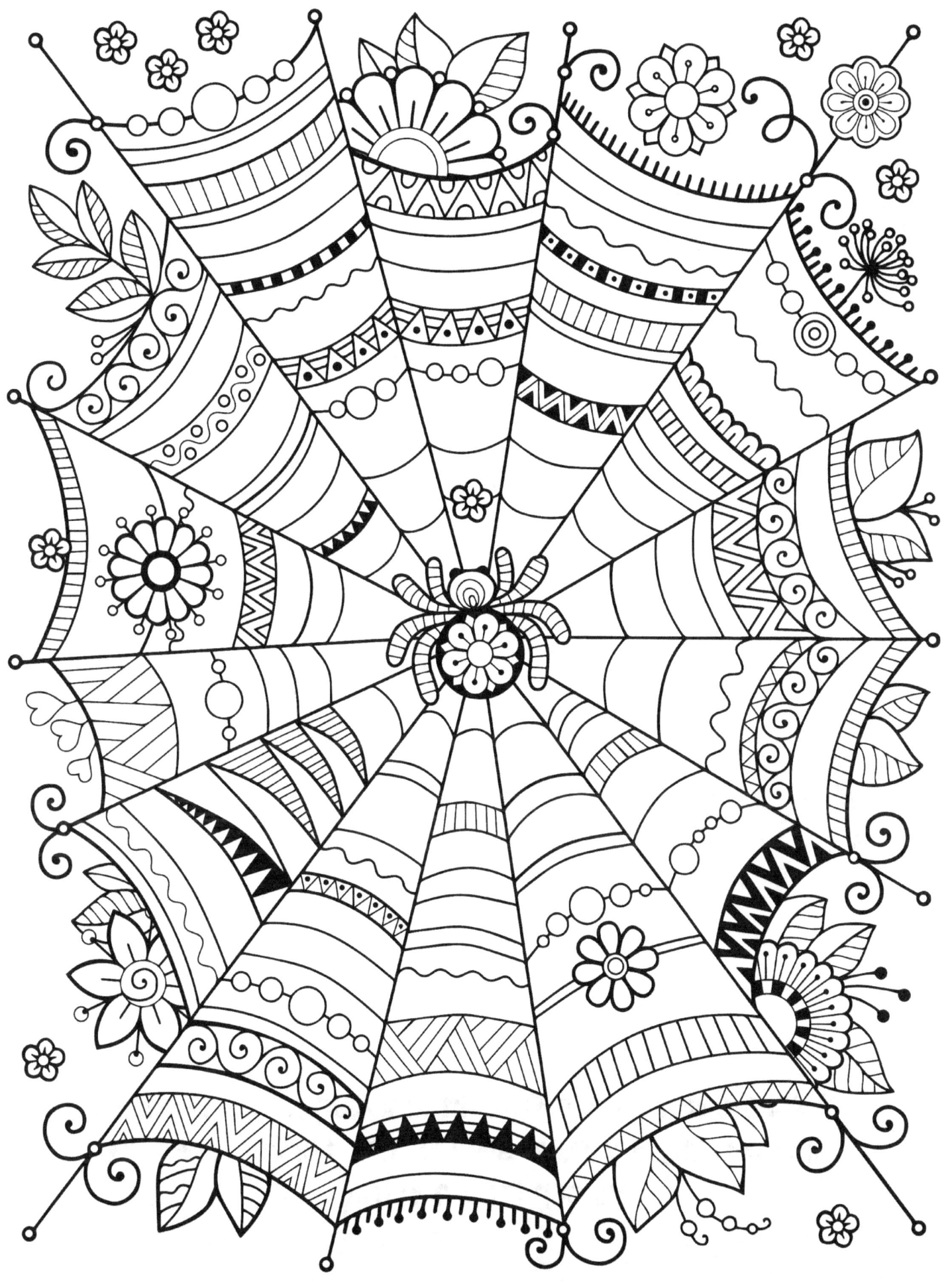

""Halloween wraps fear in innocence, as though it were a slightly sour sweet. Let terror, then, Be turned into a treat...""

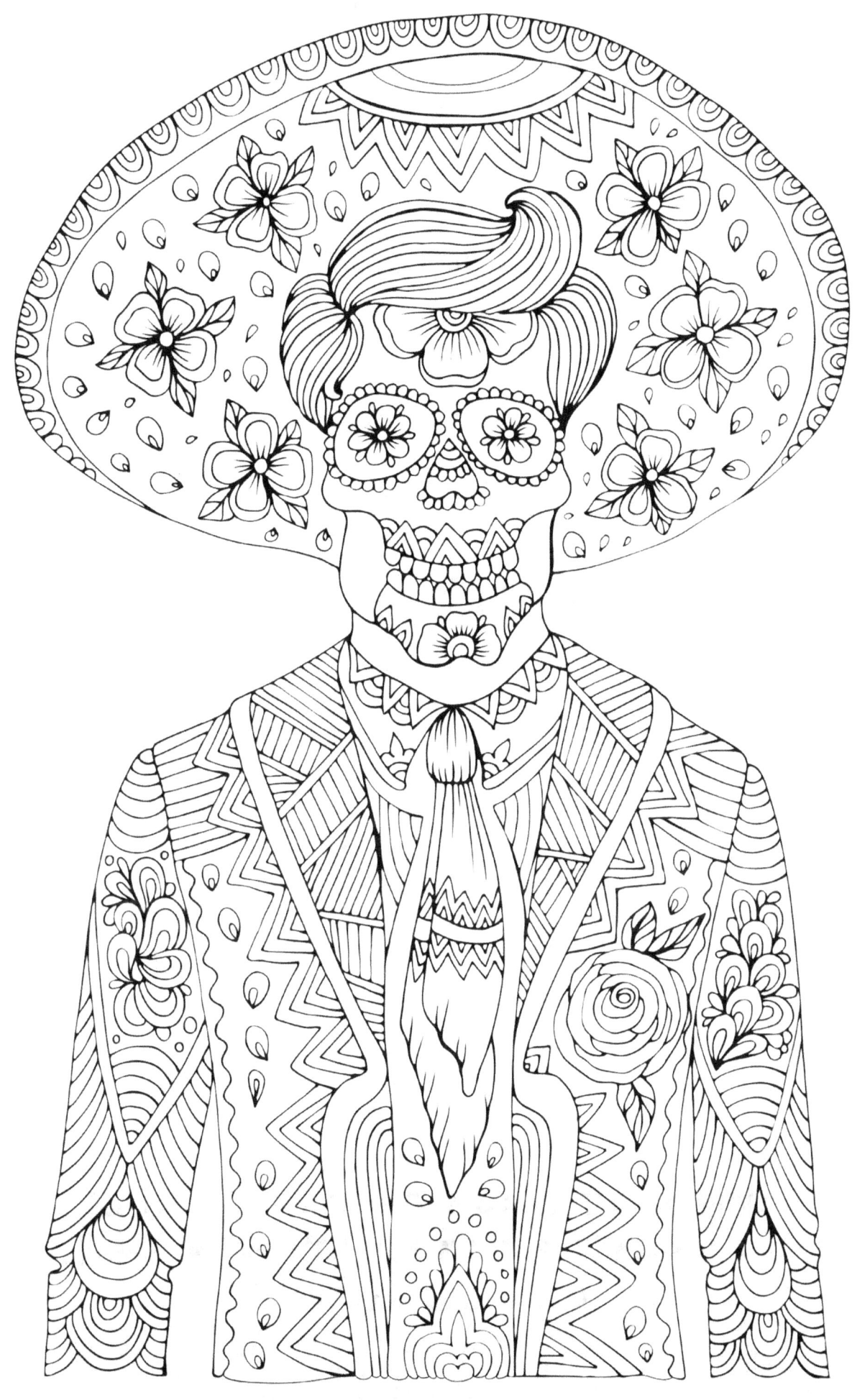

""Halloween wraps fear in innocence, as though it were a slightly sour sweet. Let terror, then, Be turned into a treat…"

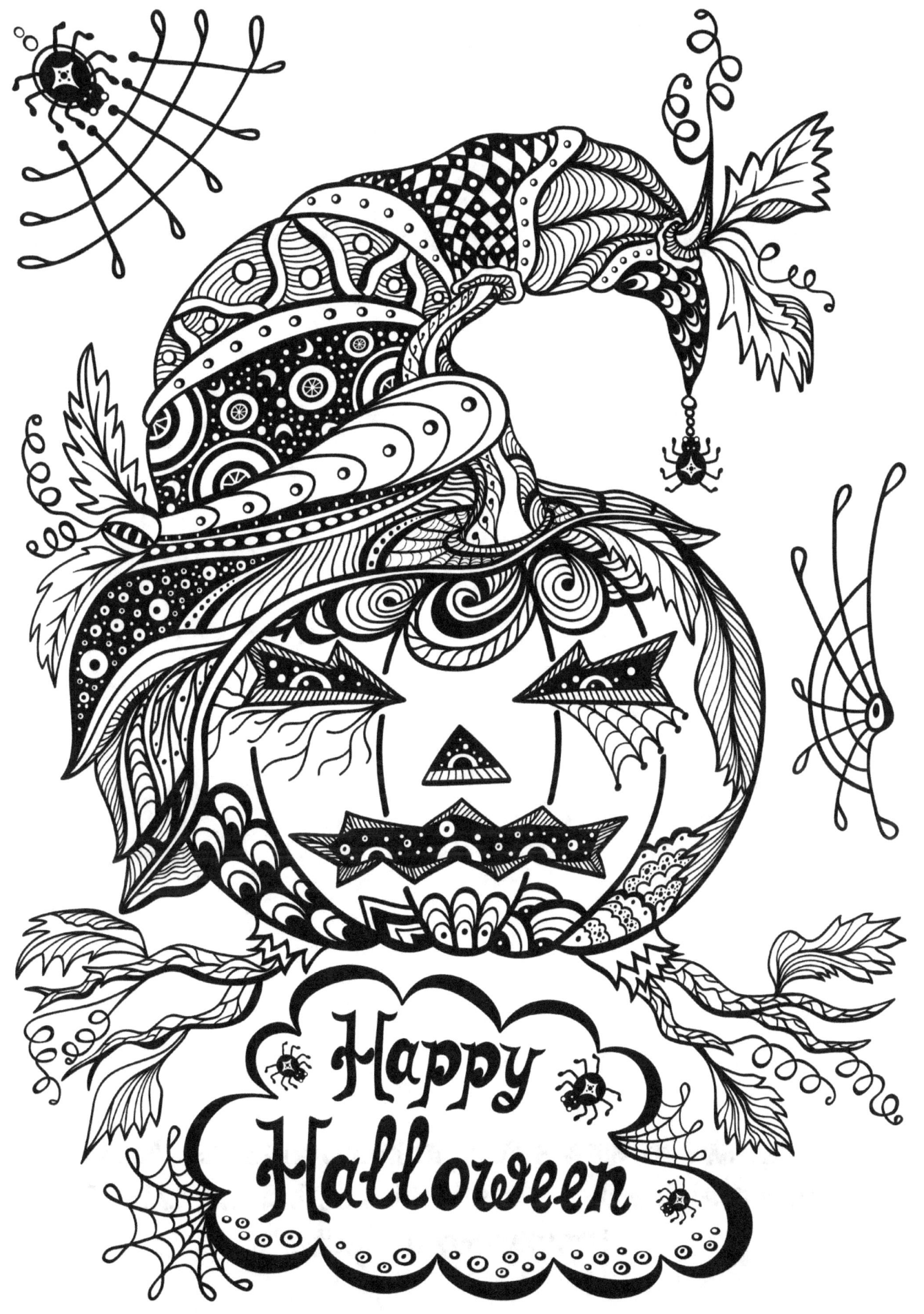

""Halloween wraps fear in innocence, as though it were a slightly sour sweet. Let terror, then, Be turneD into a treat..."

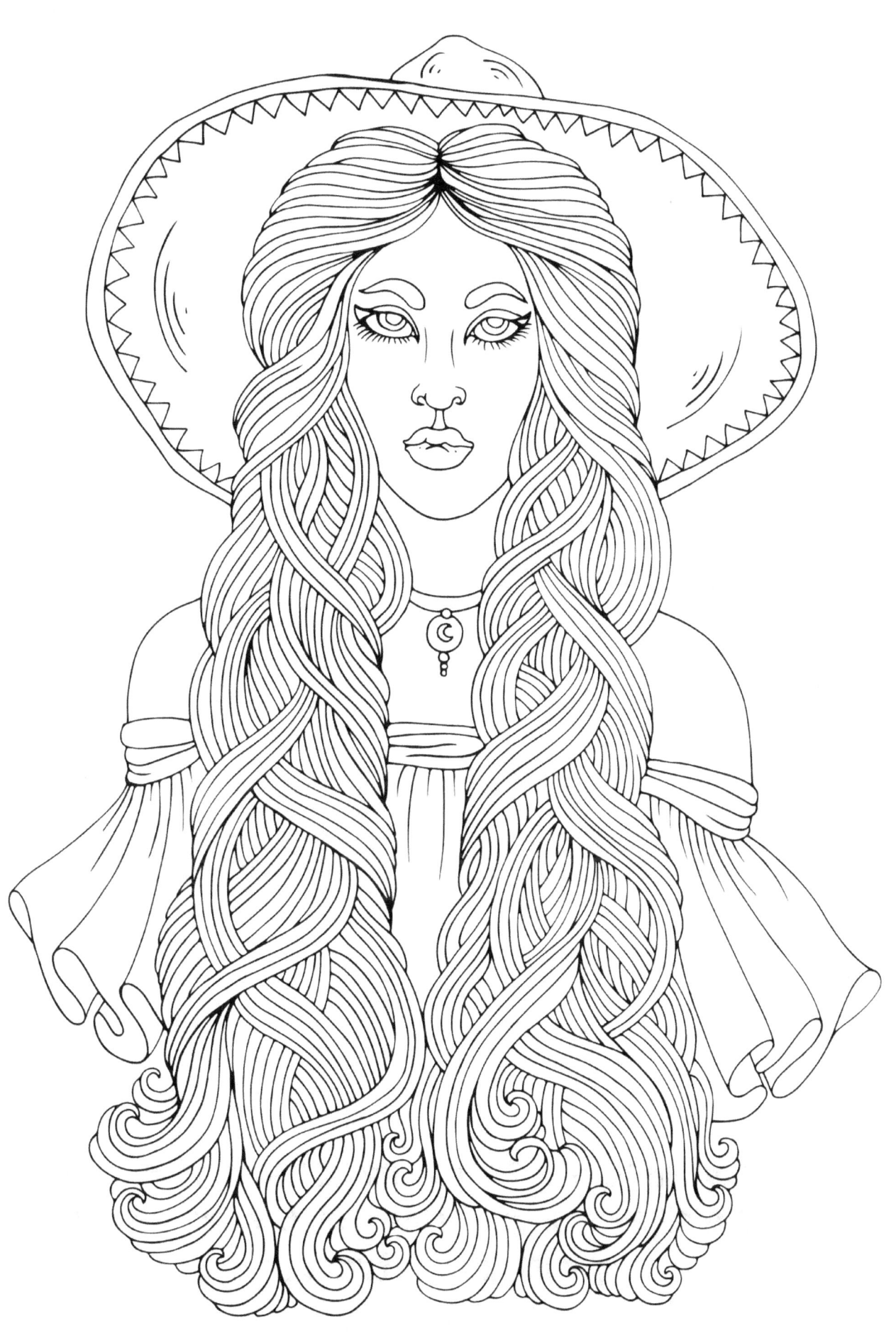

""Halloween wraps fear in innocence, as though it were a slightly sour sweet. Let terror, then, Be turned into a treat..."

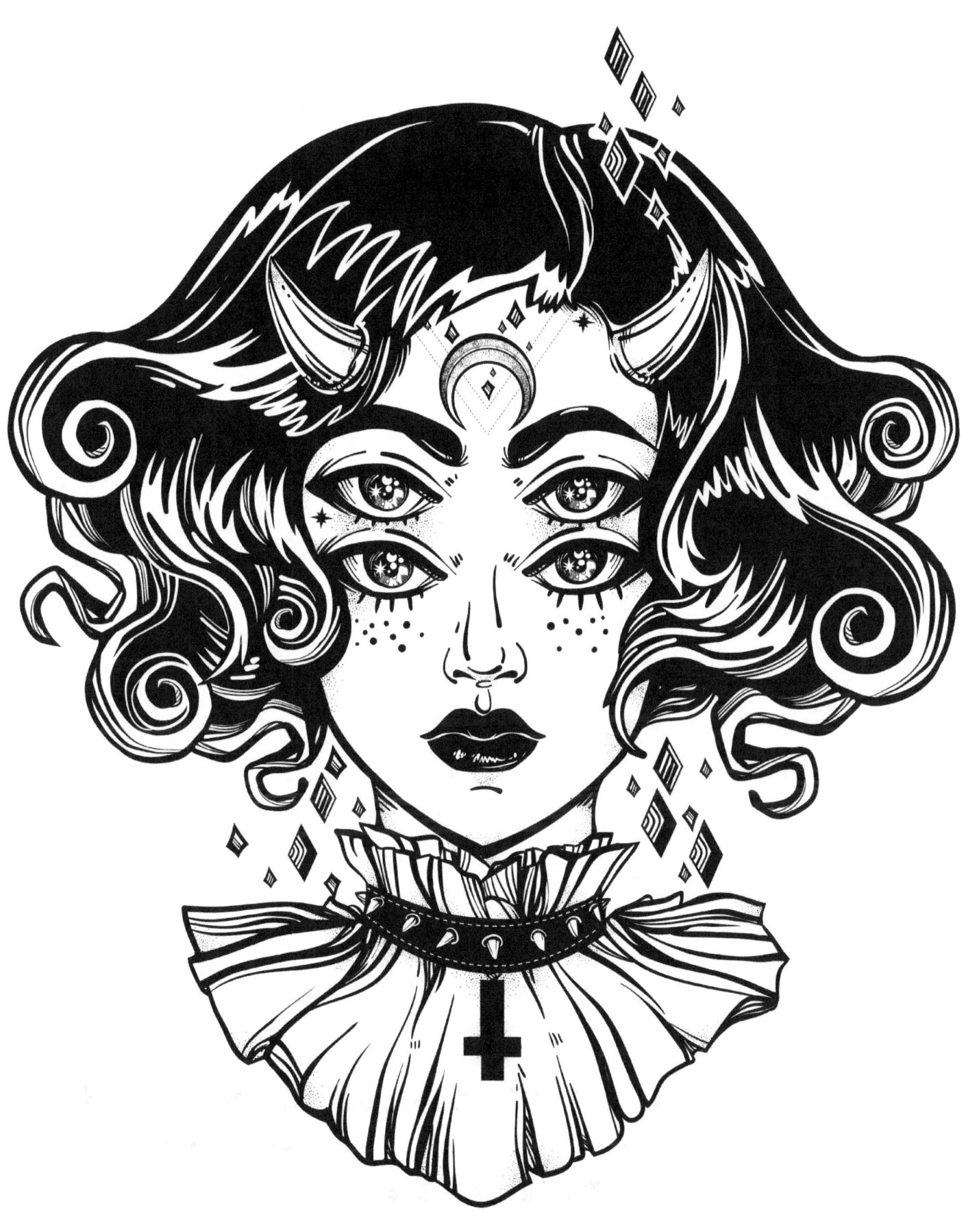

""Halloween wraps fear in innocence, as though it were a slightly sour sweet. Let terror, then, Be turned into a treat..."

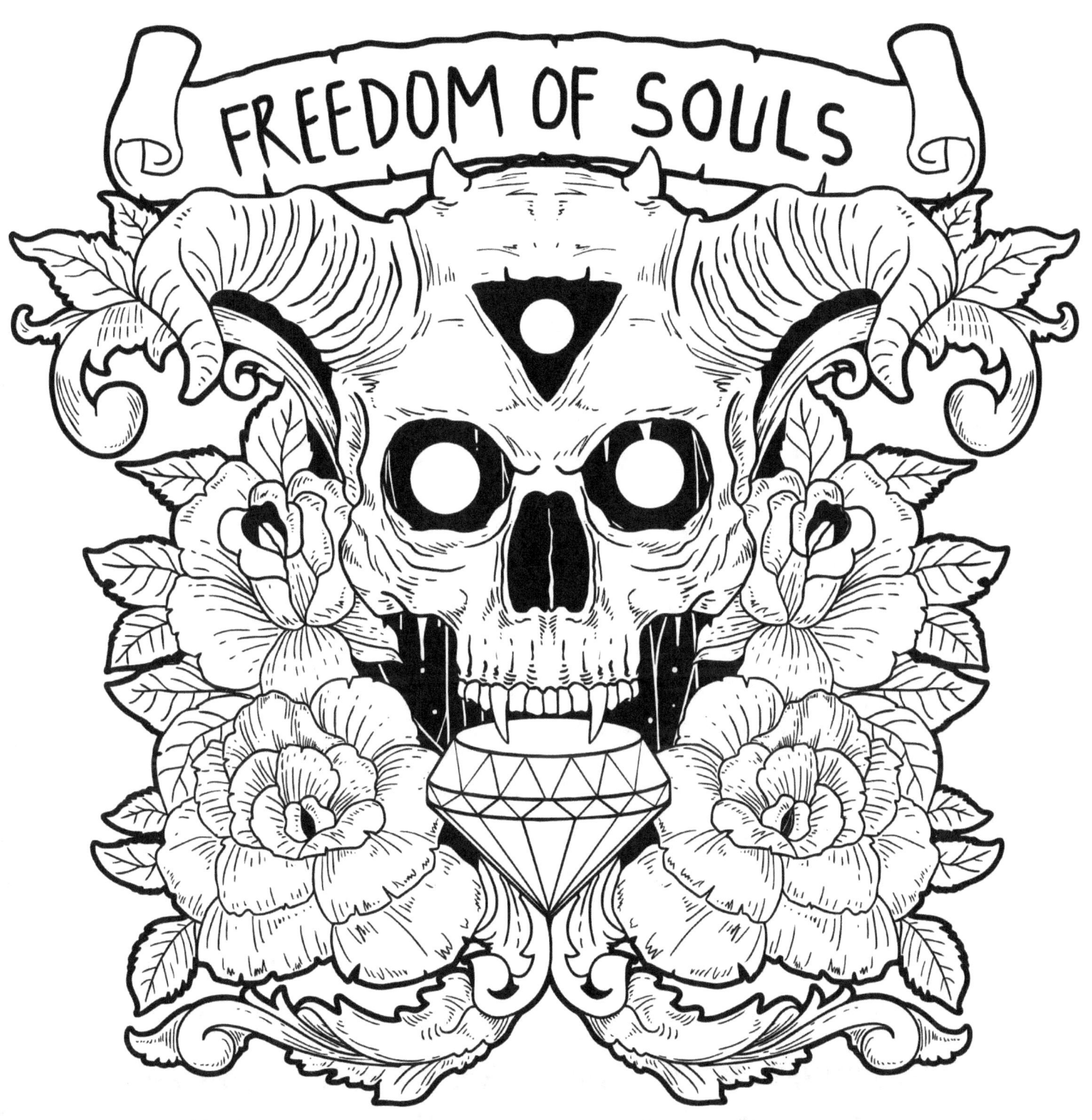

""Halloween wraps fear in innocence, as though it were a slightly sour sweet. Let terror, then, Be turned into a treat..."

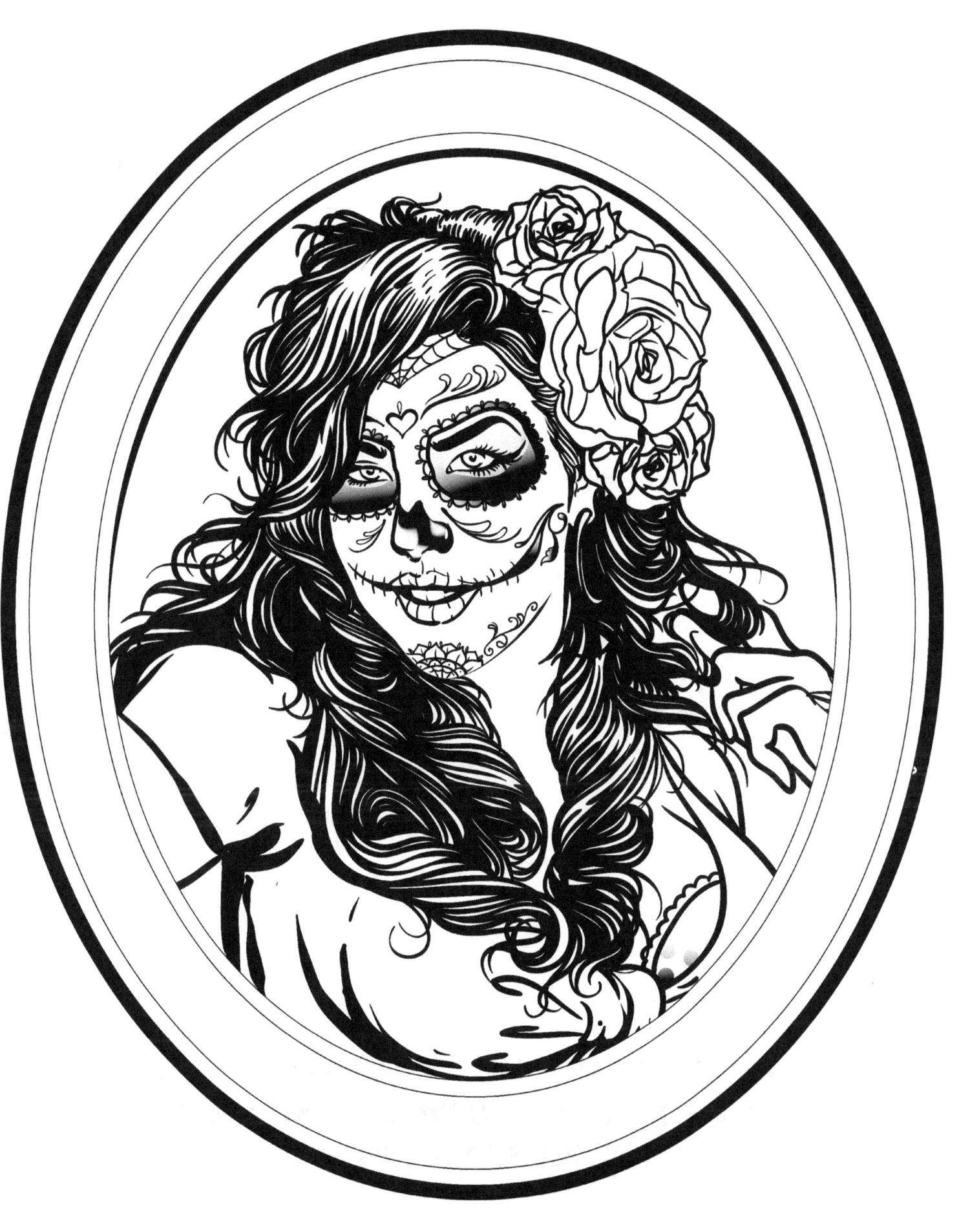

""Halloween wraps fear in innocence, as though it were a slightly sour sweet. Let terror, then, Be turned into a treat...""

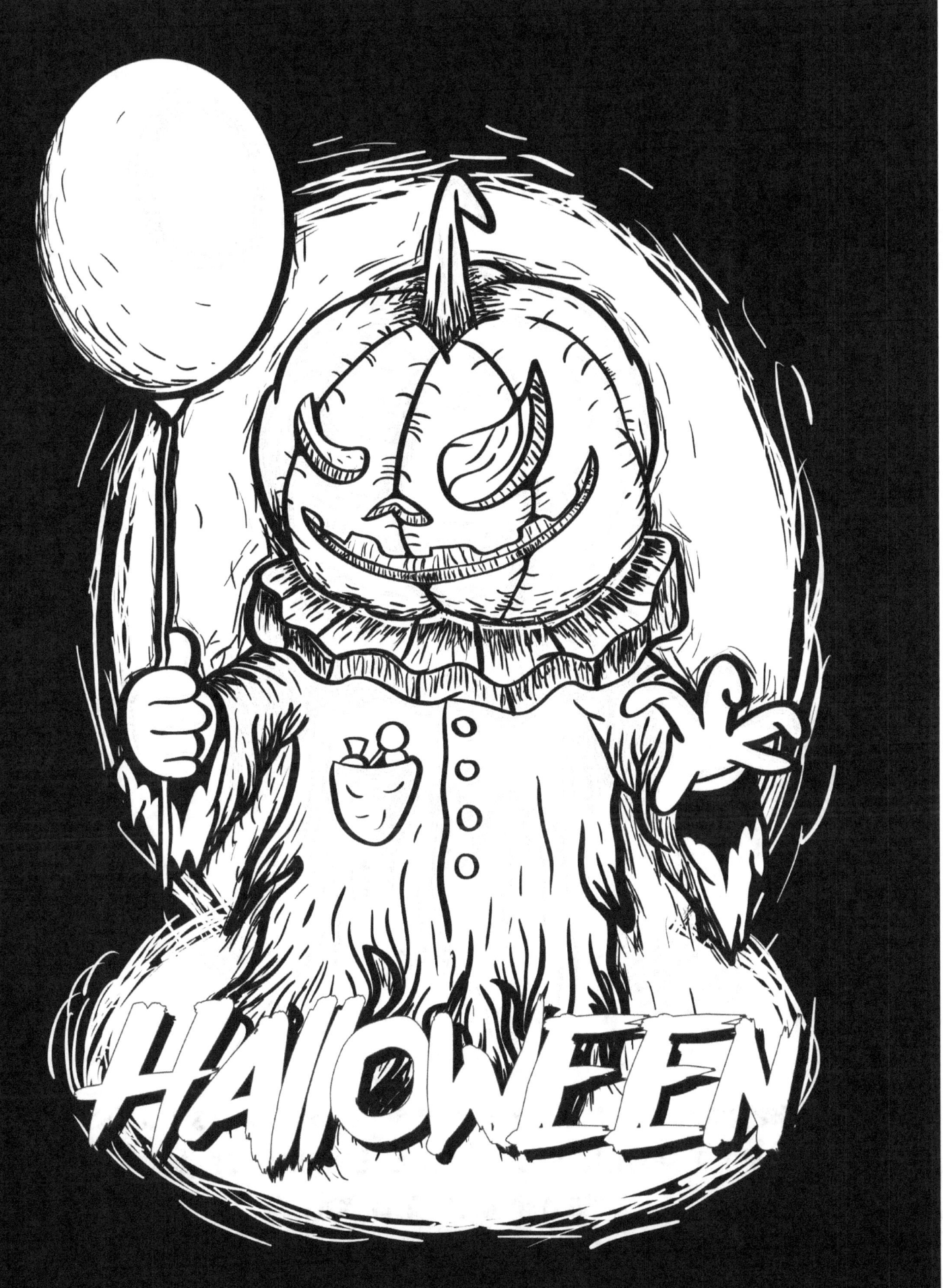

""Halloween wraps fear in innocence, as though it were a slightly sour sweet. Let terror, then, Be turned into a treat..."

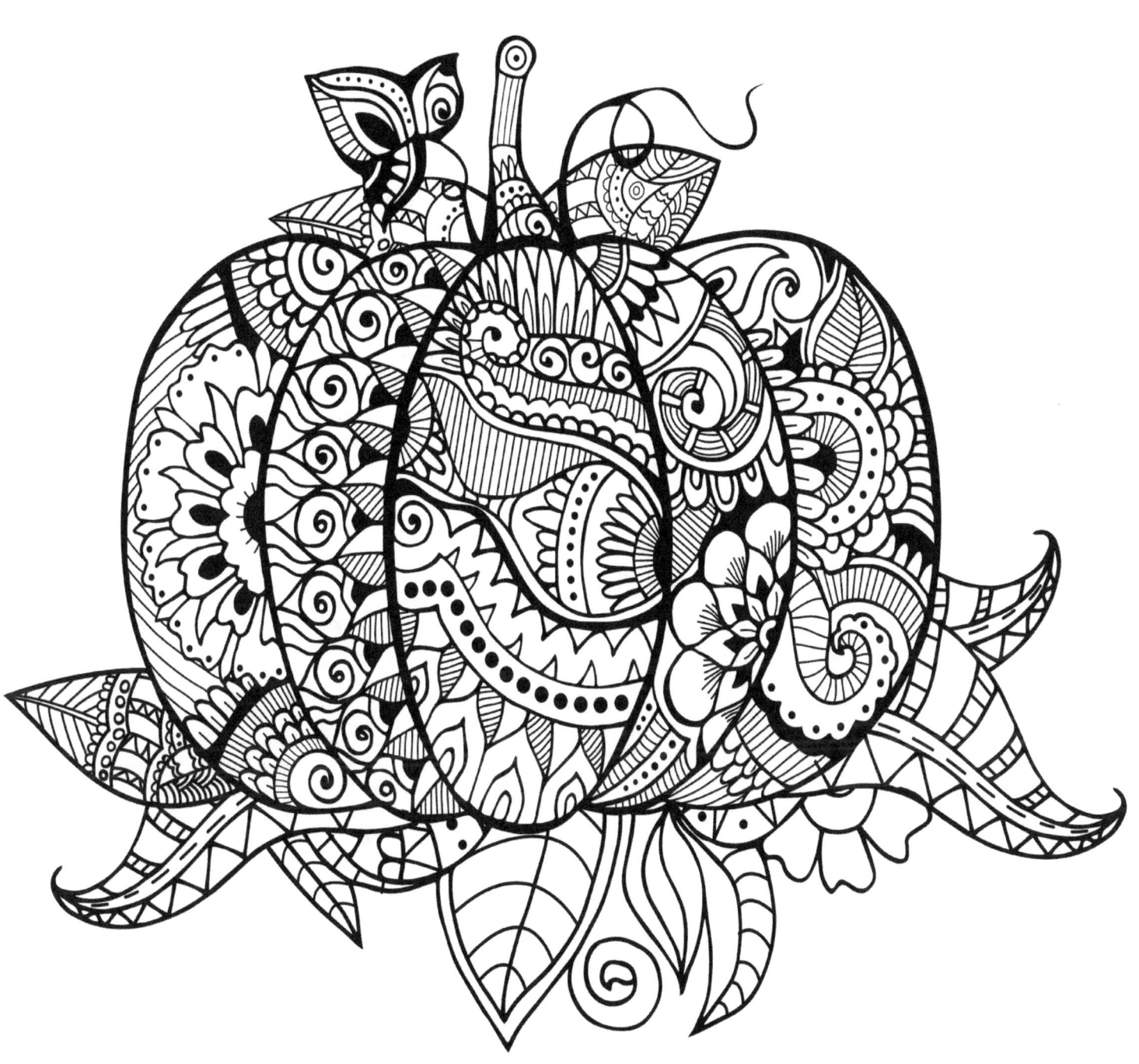

""Halloween wraps fear in innocence, as though it were a slightly sour sweet. Let terror, then, Be turneD into a treat..."

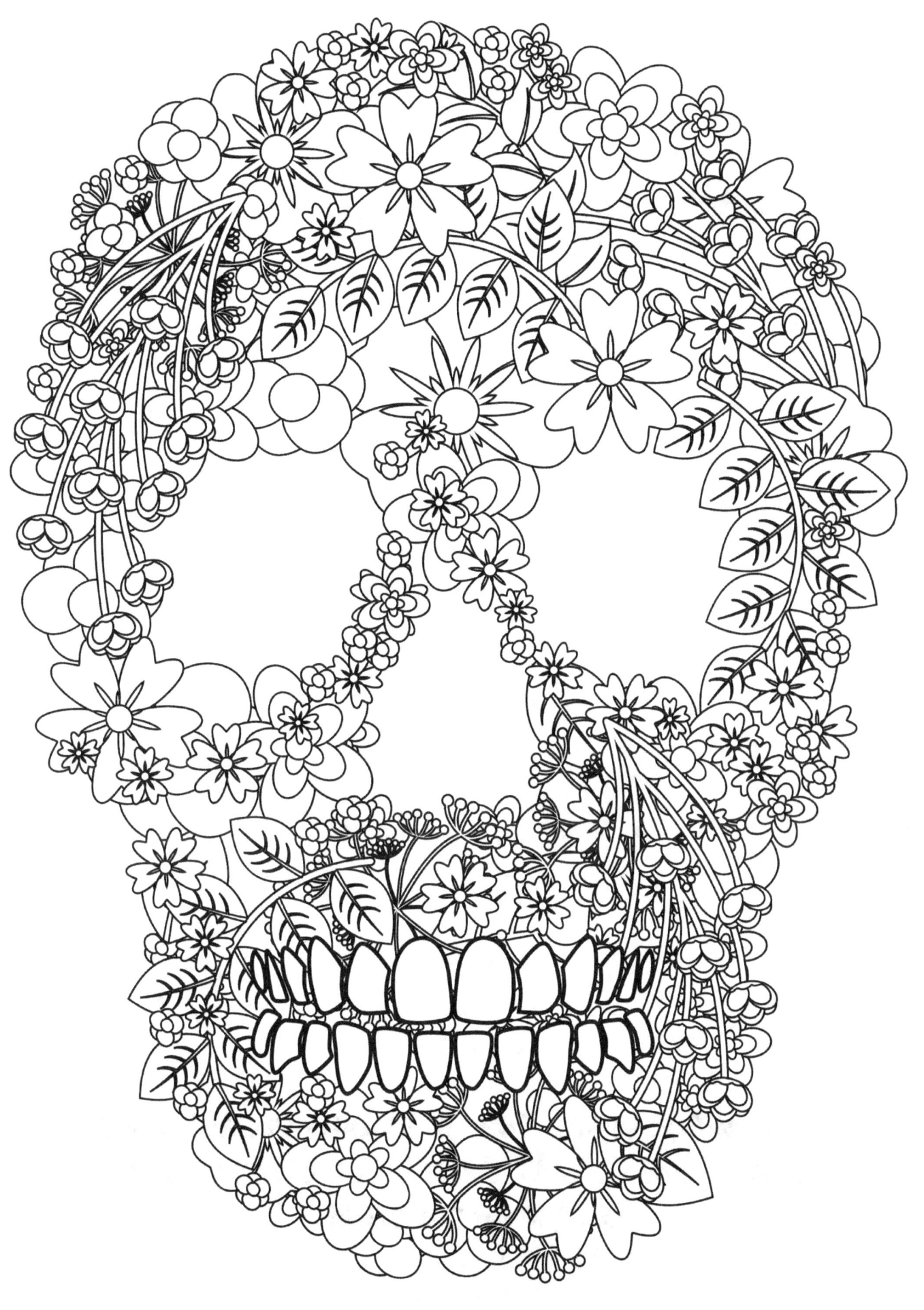

""Halloween wraps fear in innocence, as though it were a slightly sour sweet. Let terror, then, Be turned into a treat..."

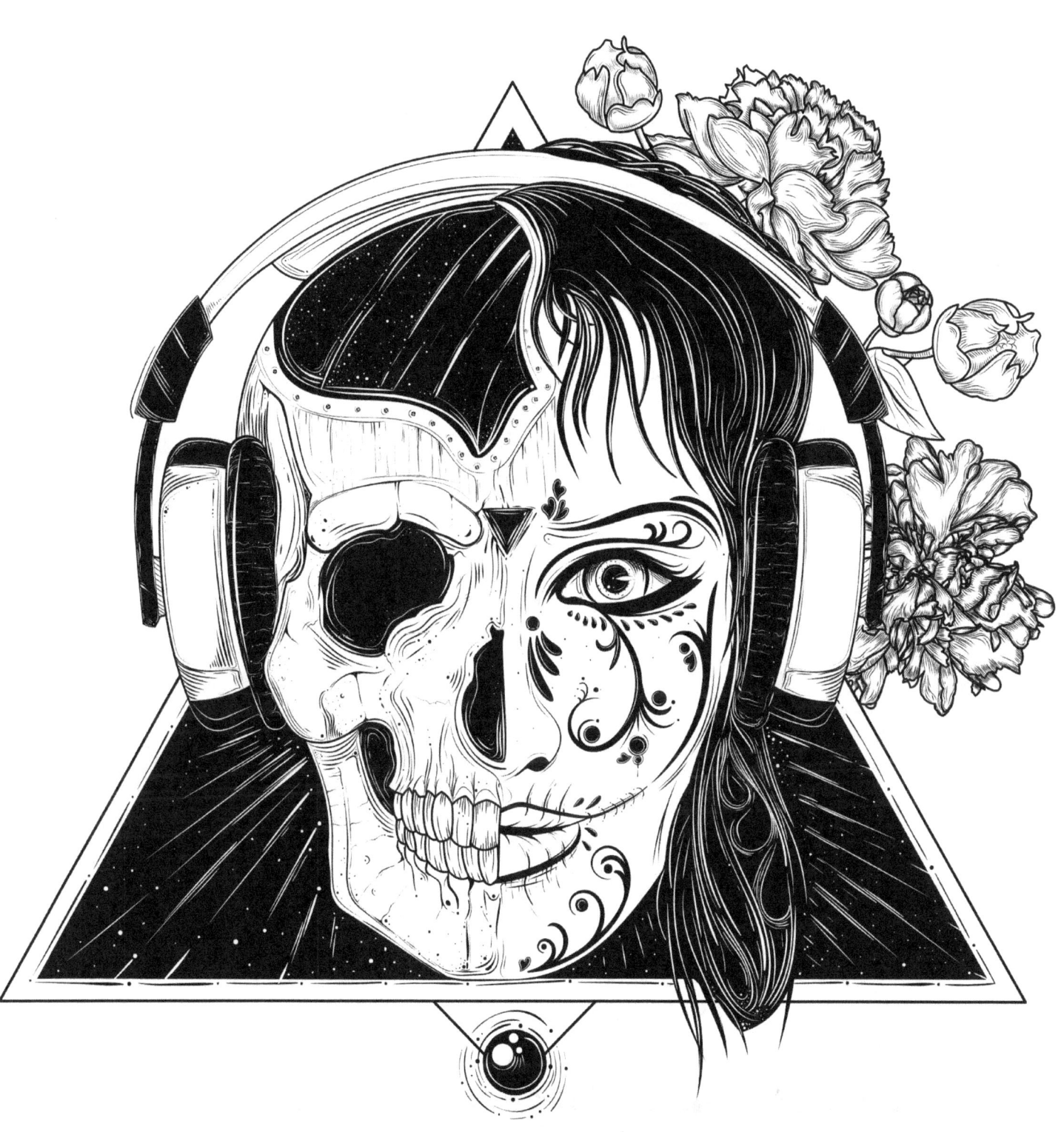

""Halloween wraps fear in innocence, as though it were a slightly sour sweet. Let terror, then, Be turneD into a treat…"

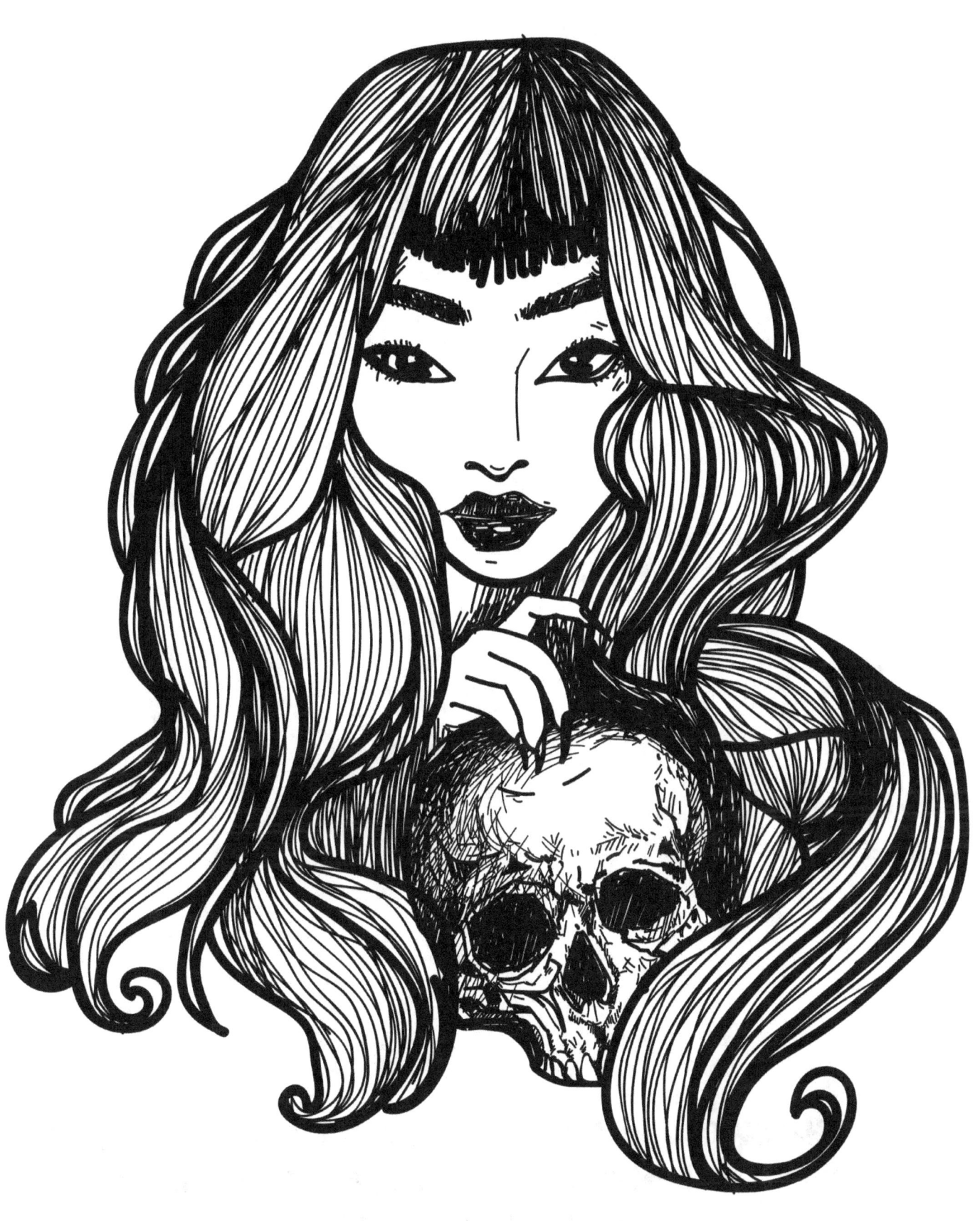

""Halloween wraps fear in innocence, as though it were a slightly sour sweet. Let terror, then, Be turned into a treat..."

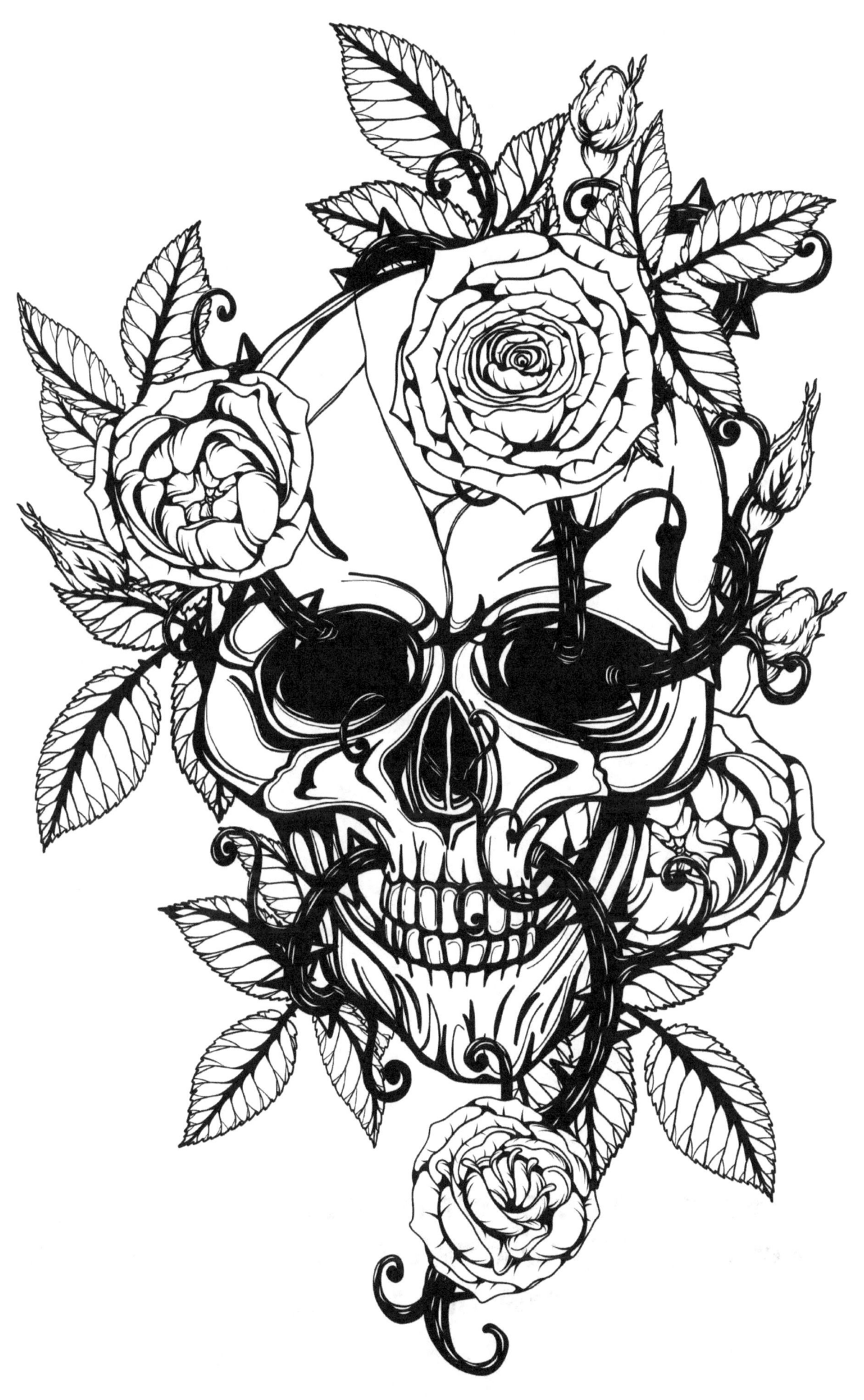

""Halloween wraps fear in innocence, as though it were a slightly sour sweet. Let terror, then, Be turned into a treat...""

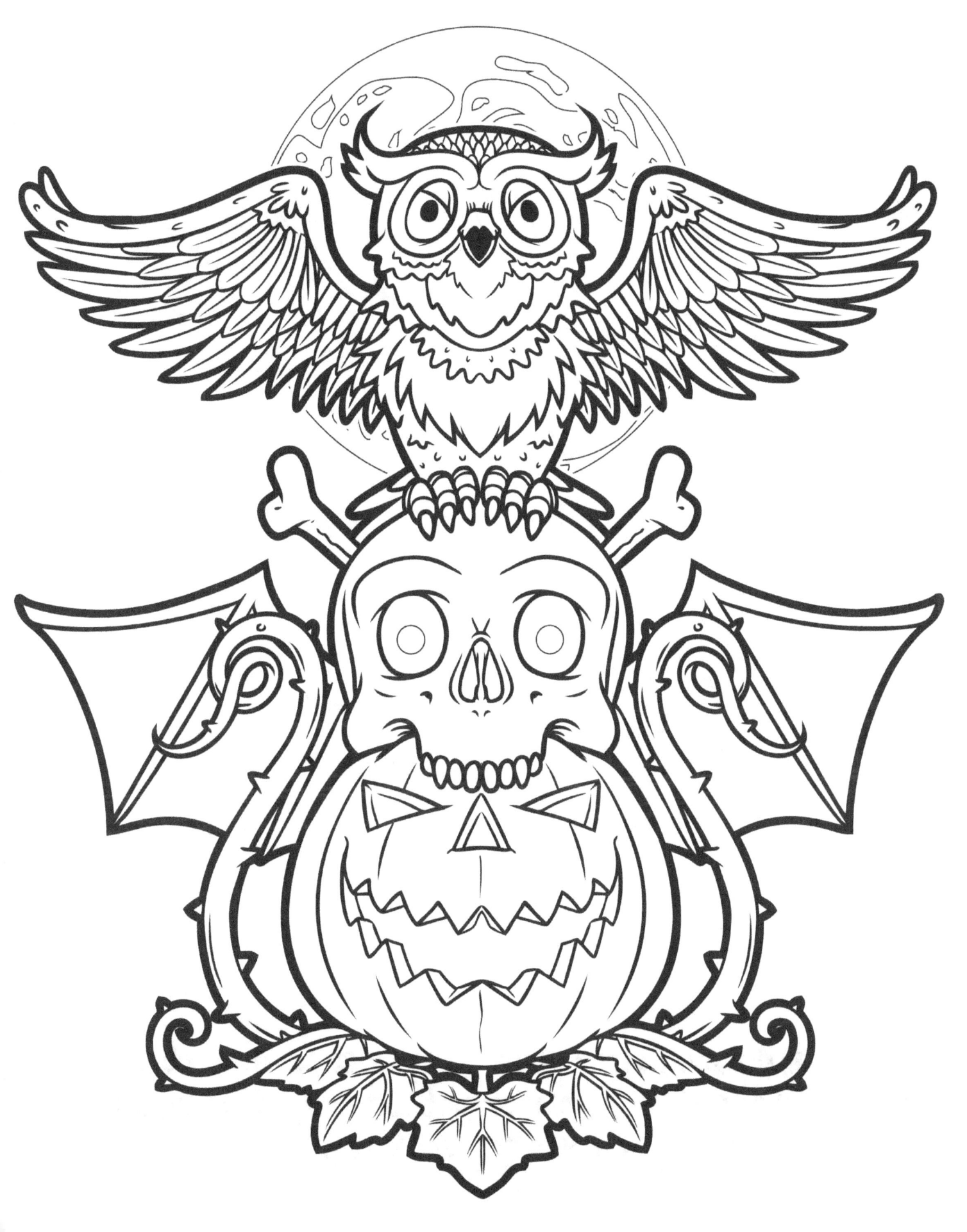

""Halloween wraps fear in innocence, as though it were a slightly sour sweet. Let terror, then, Be turned into a treat...""

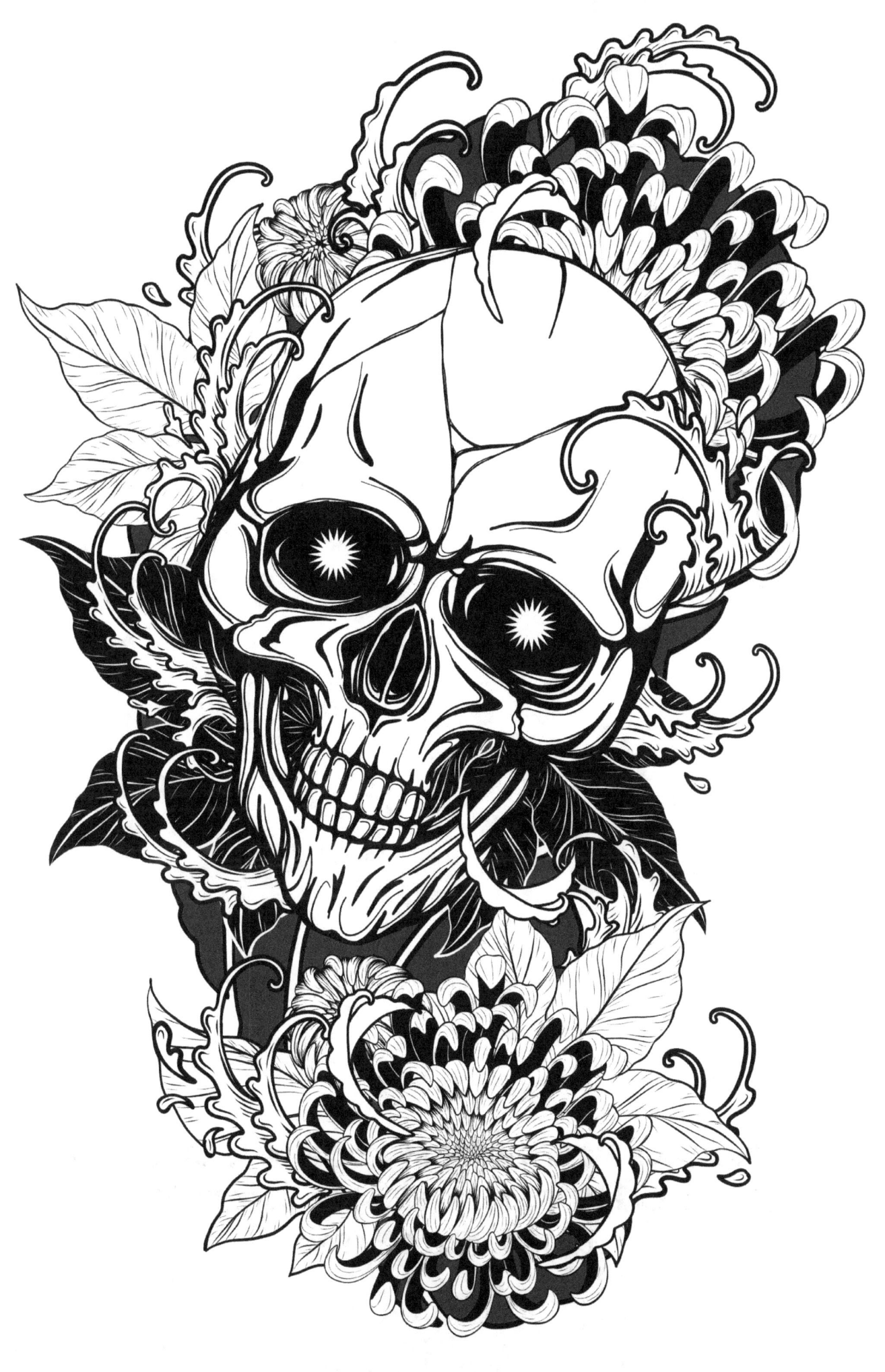

""Halloween wraps fear in innocence, as though it were a slightly sour sweet. Let terror, then, Be turned into a treat..."

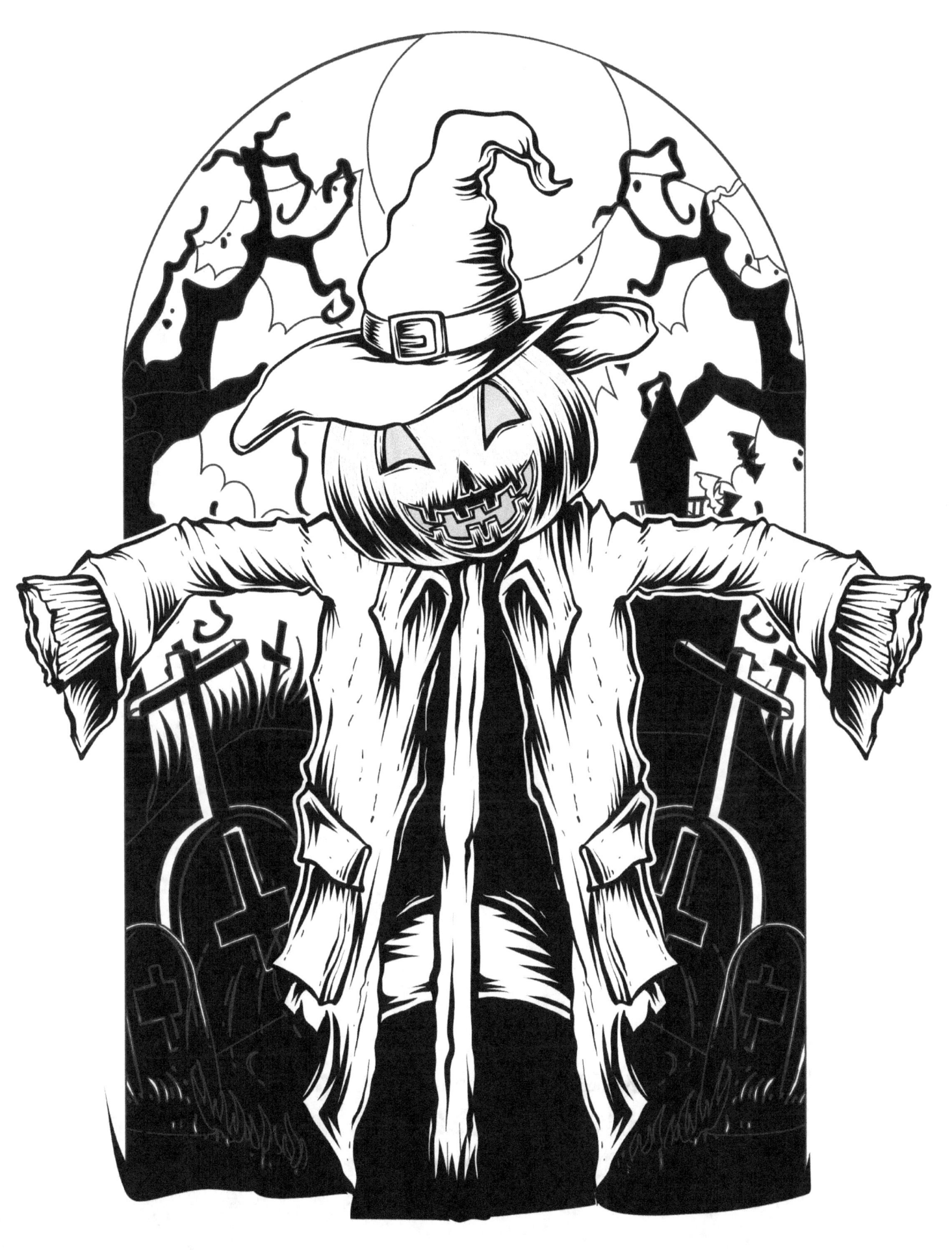

""Halloween wraps fear in innocence, as though it were a slightly sour sweet. Let terror, then, Be turned into a treat...""

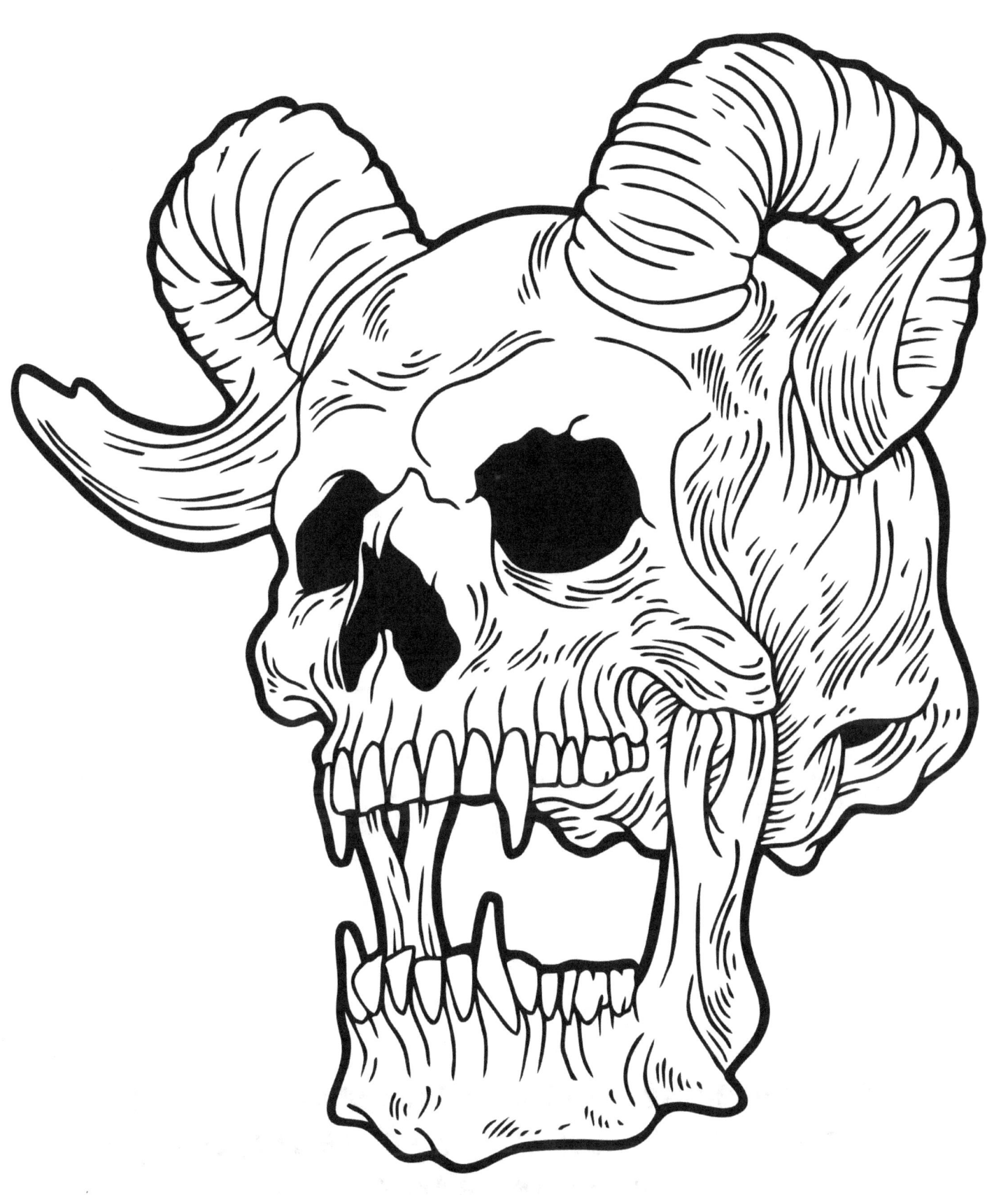

""Halloween wraps fear in innocence, as though it were a slightly sour sweet. Let terror, then, Be turneD into a treat...""

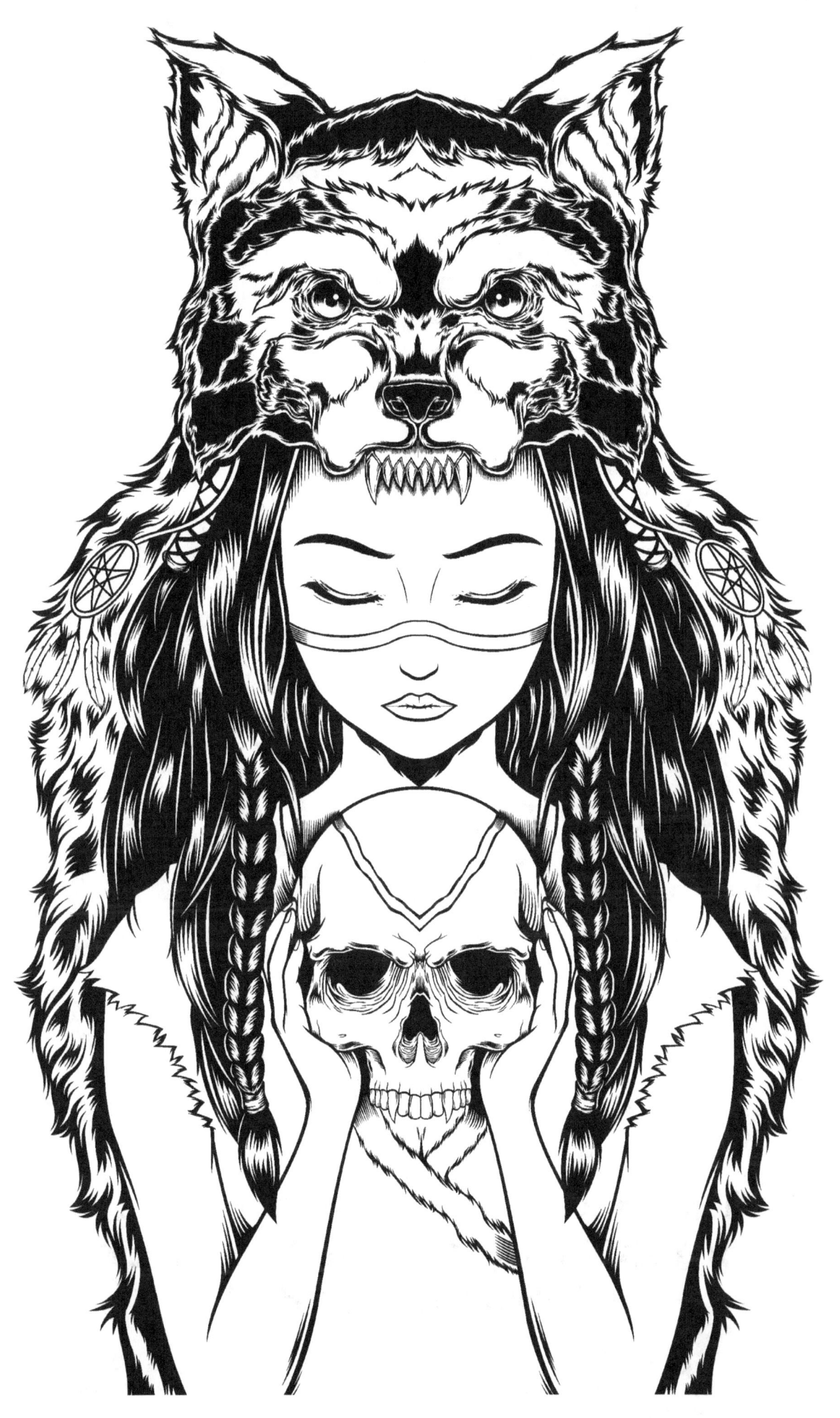

""Halloween wraps fear in innocence, as though it were a slightly sour sweet. Let terror, then, Be turned into a treat..."

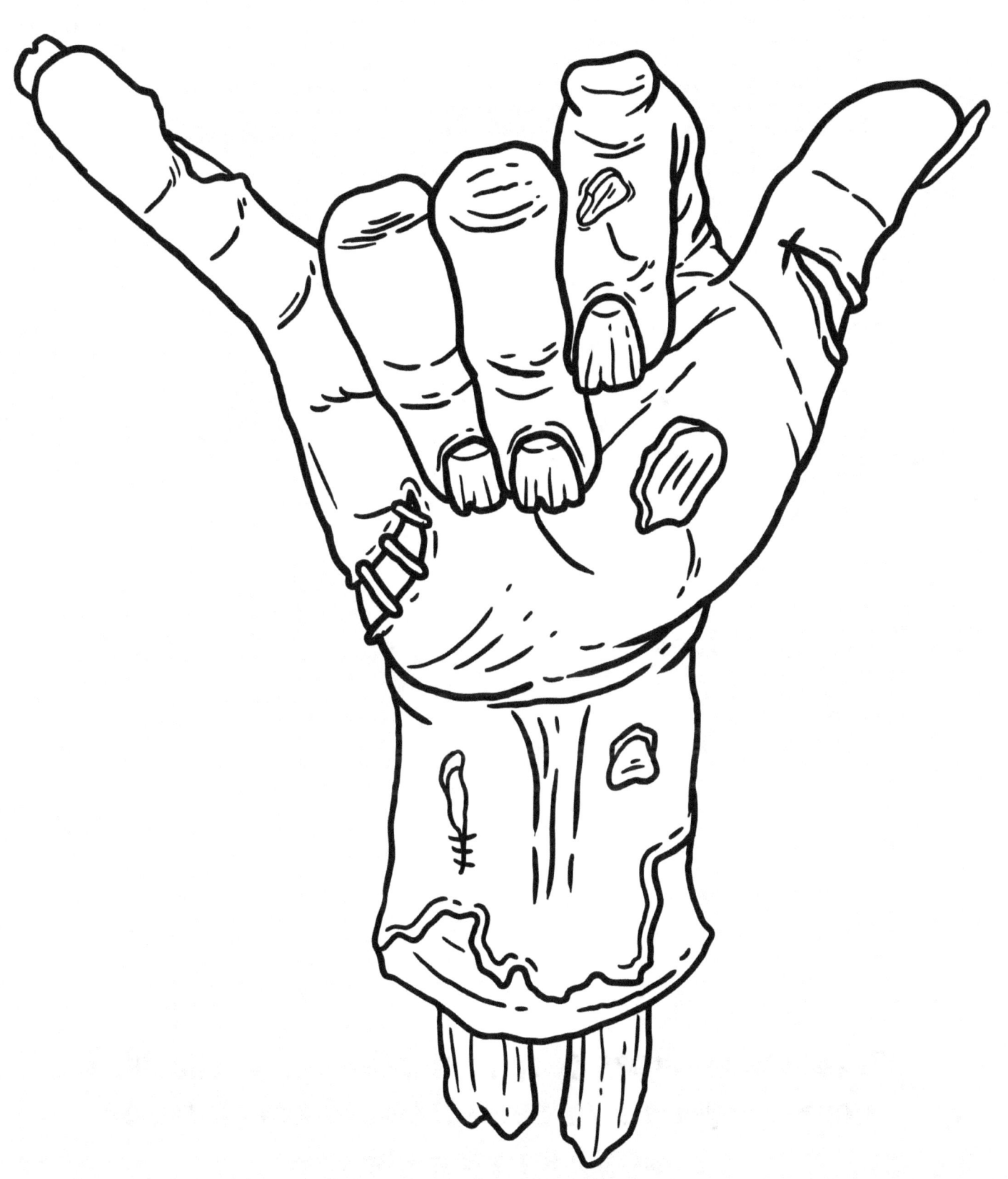

""Halloween wraps fear in innocence, as though it were a slightly sour sweet. Let terror, then, Be turneD into a treat…"

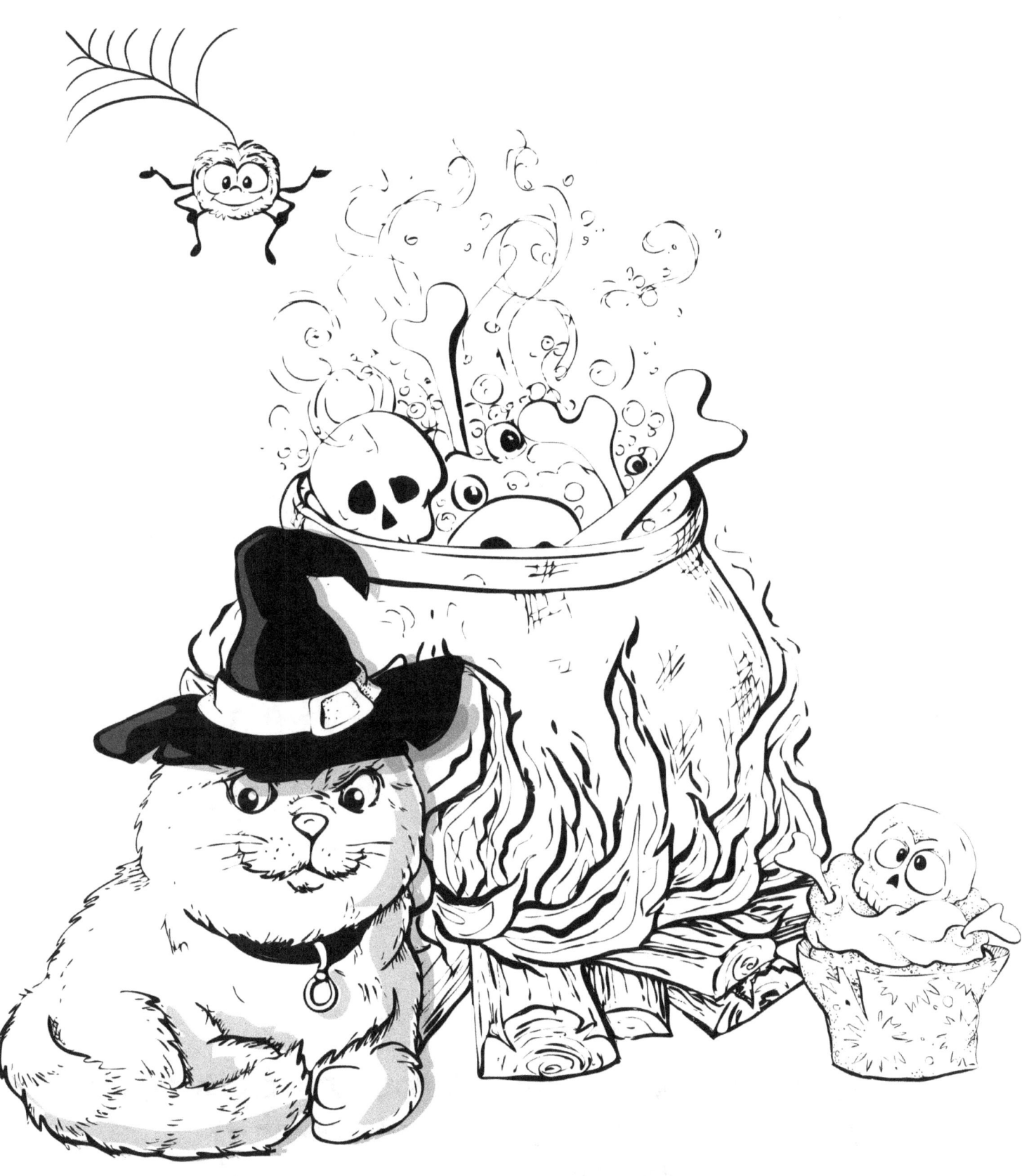

""Halloween wraps fear in innocence, as though it were a slightly sour sweet. Let terror, then, Be turned into a treat..."

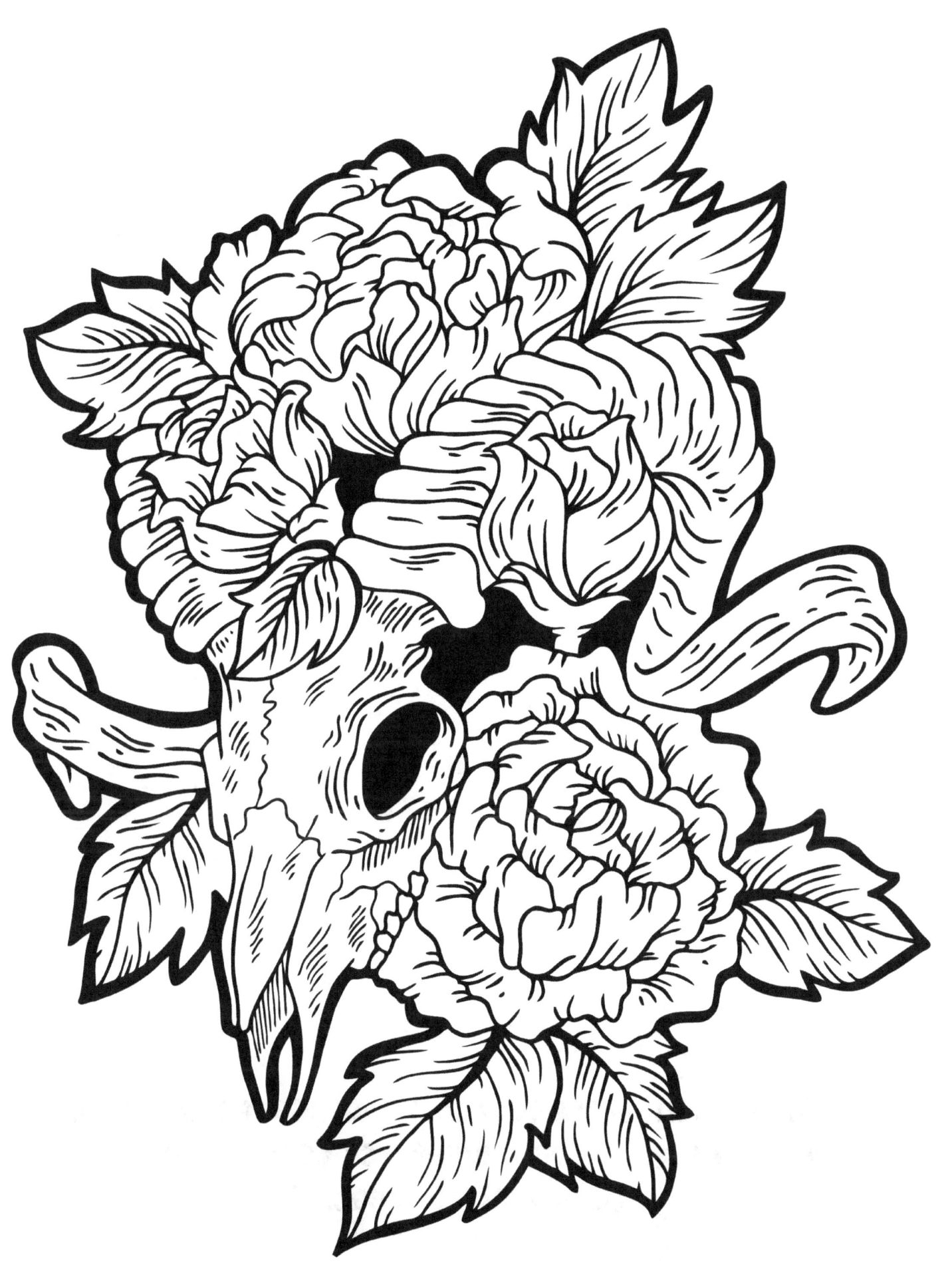

""Halloween wraps fear in innocence, as though it were a slightly sour sweet. Let terror, then, Be turned into a treat..."

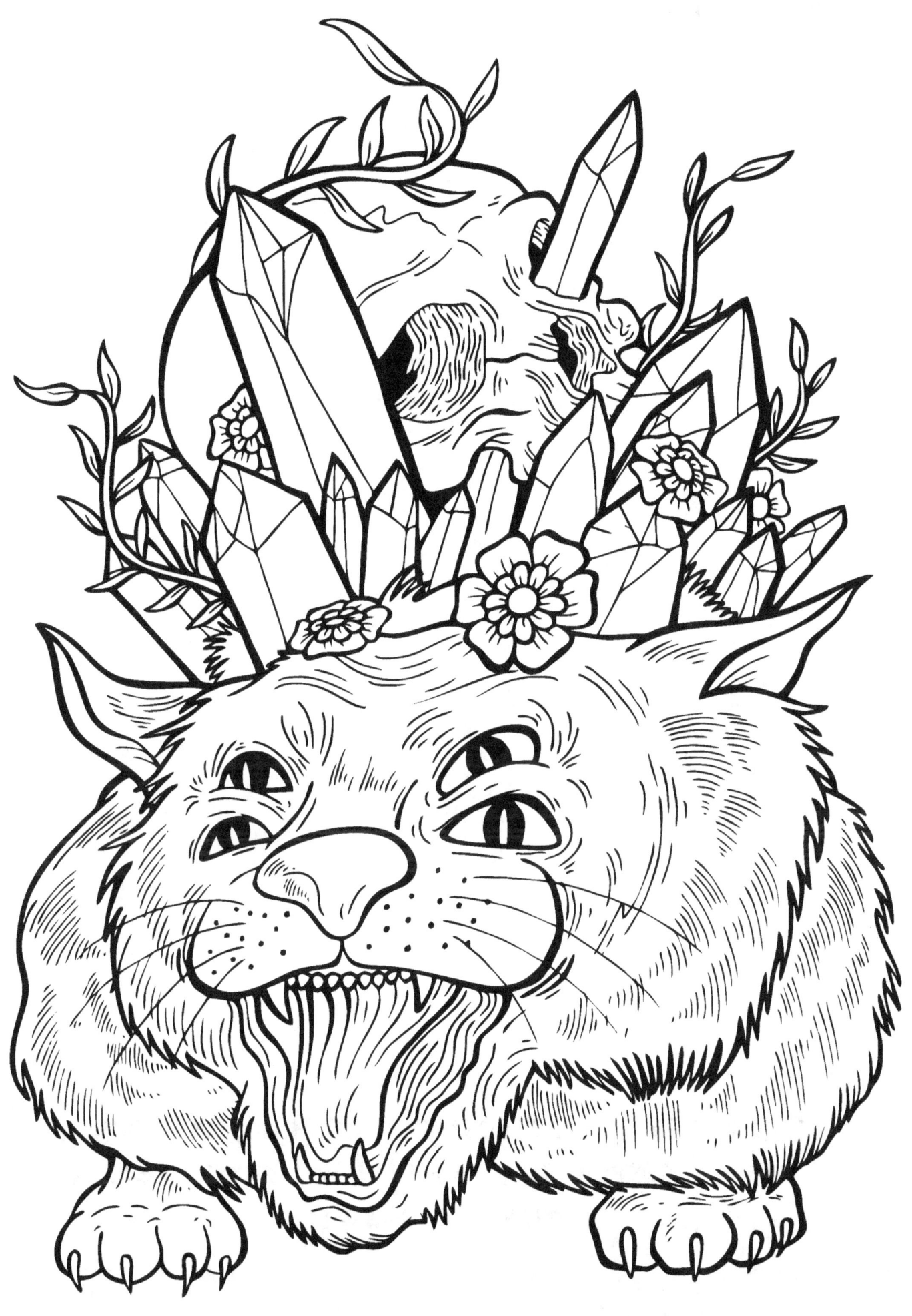

""Halloween wraps fear in innocence, as though it were a slightly sour sweet. Let terror, then, Be turned into a treat...""

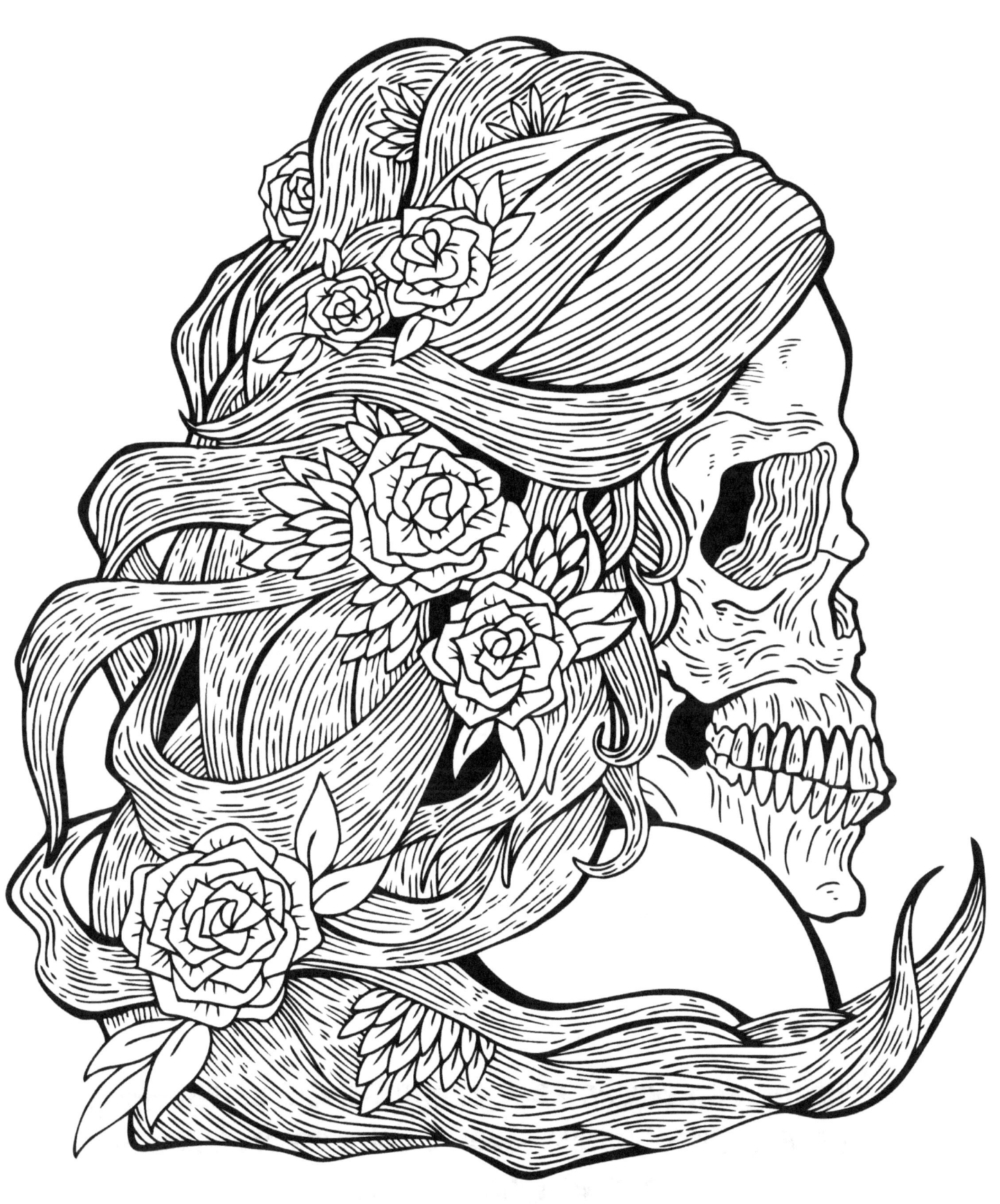

""Halloween wraps fear in innocence, as though it were a slightly sour sweet. Let terror, then, Be turned into a treat…"

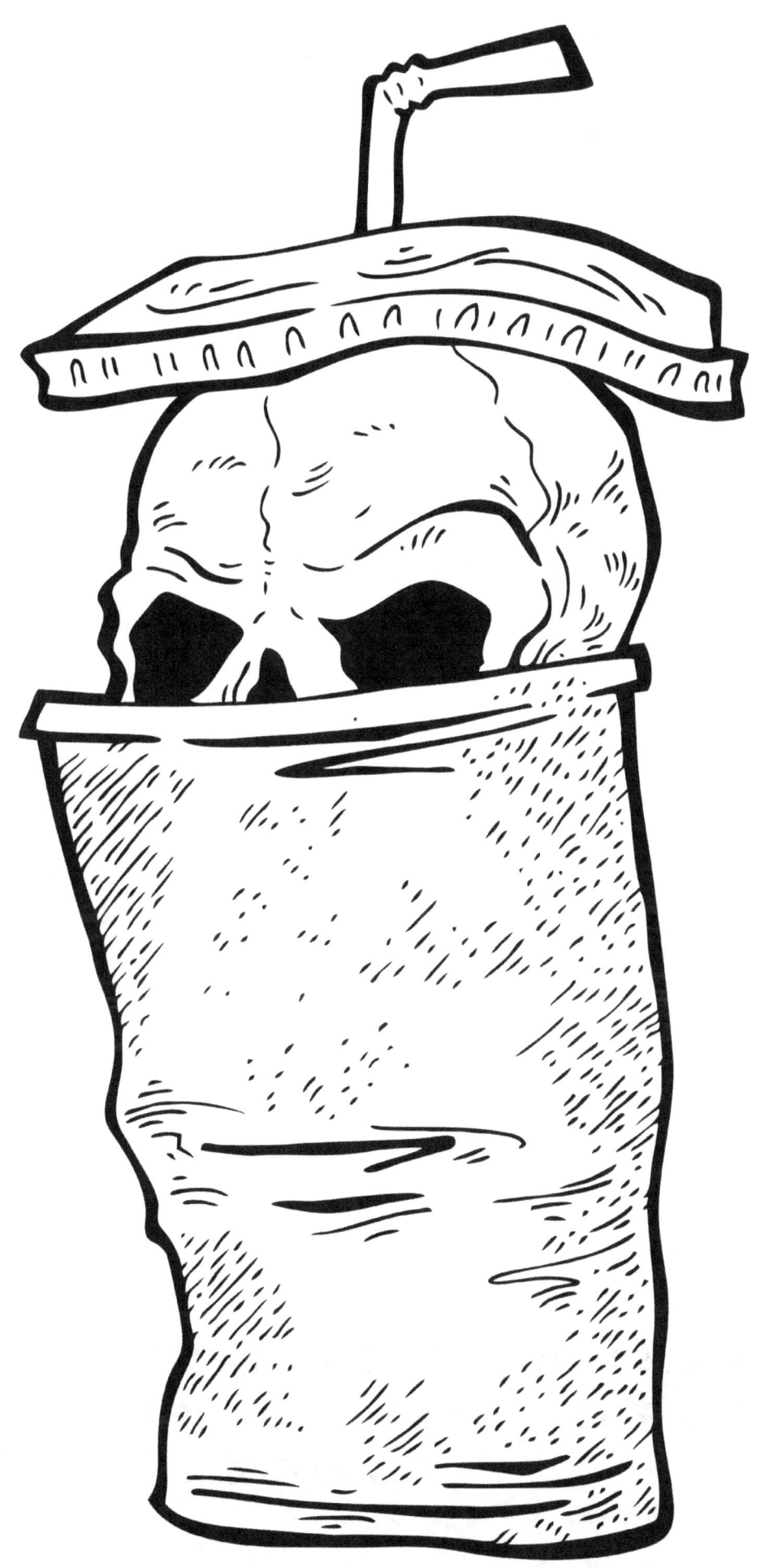

""Halloween wraps fear in innocence, as though it were a slightly sour sweet. Let terror, then, Be turned into a treat..."

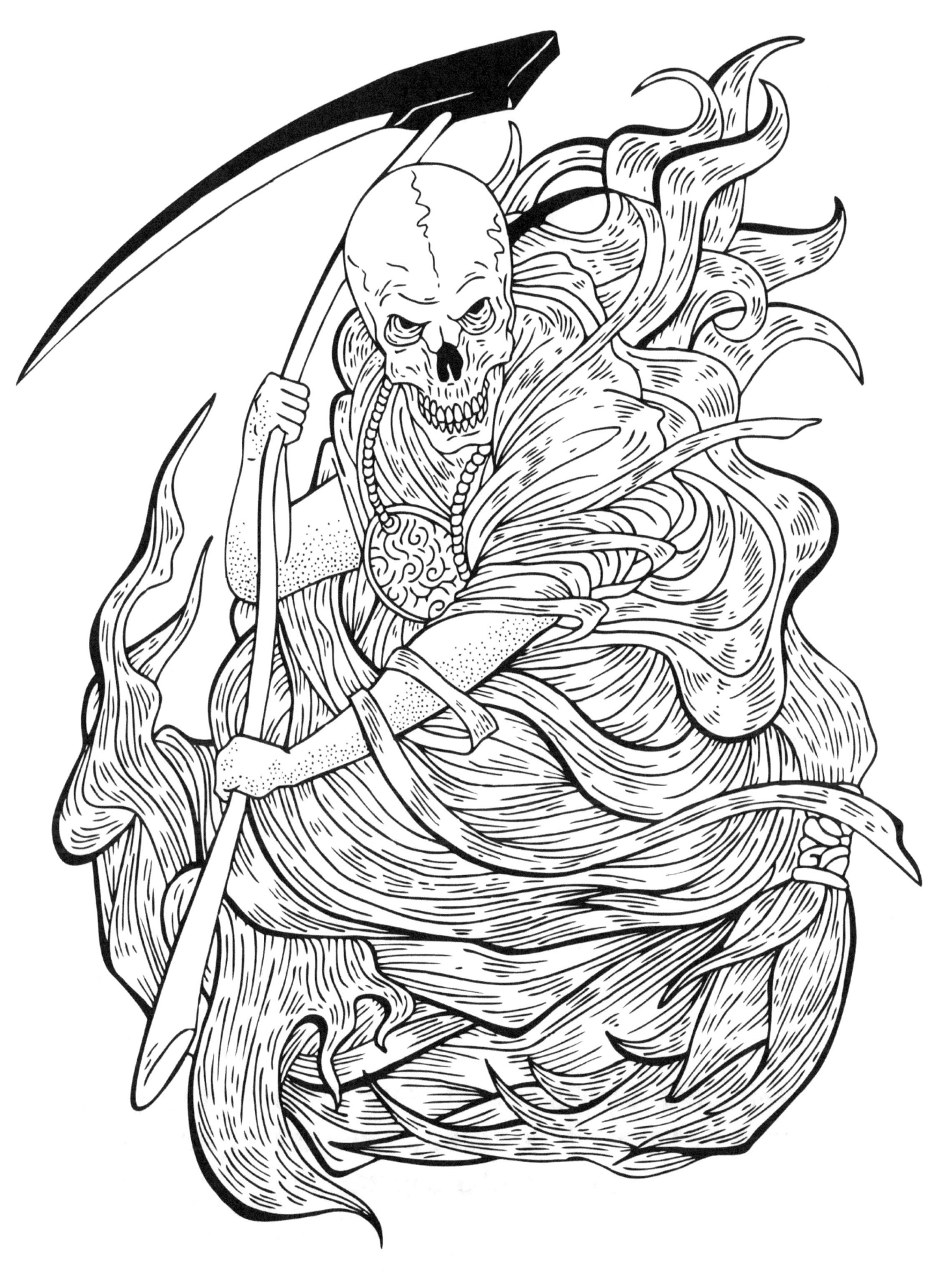

""Halloween wraps fear in innocence, as though it were a slightly sour sweet. Let terror, then, Be turneD into a treat..."

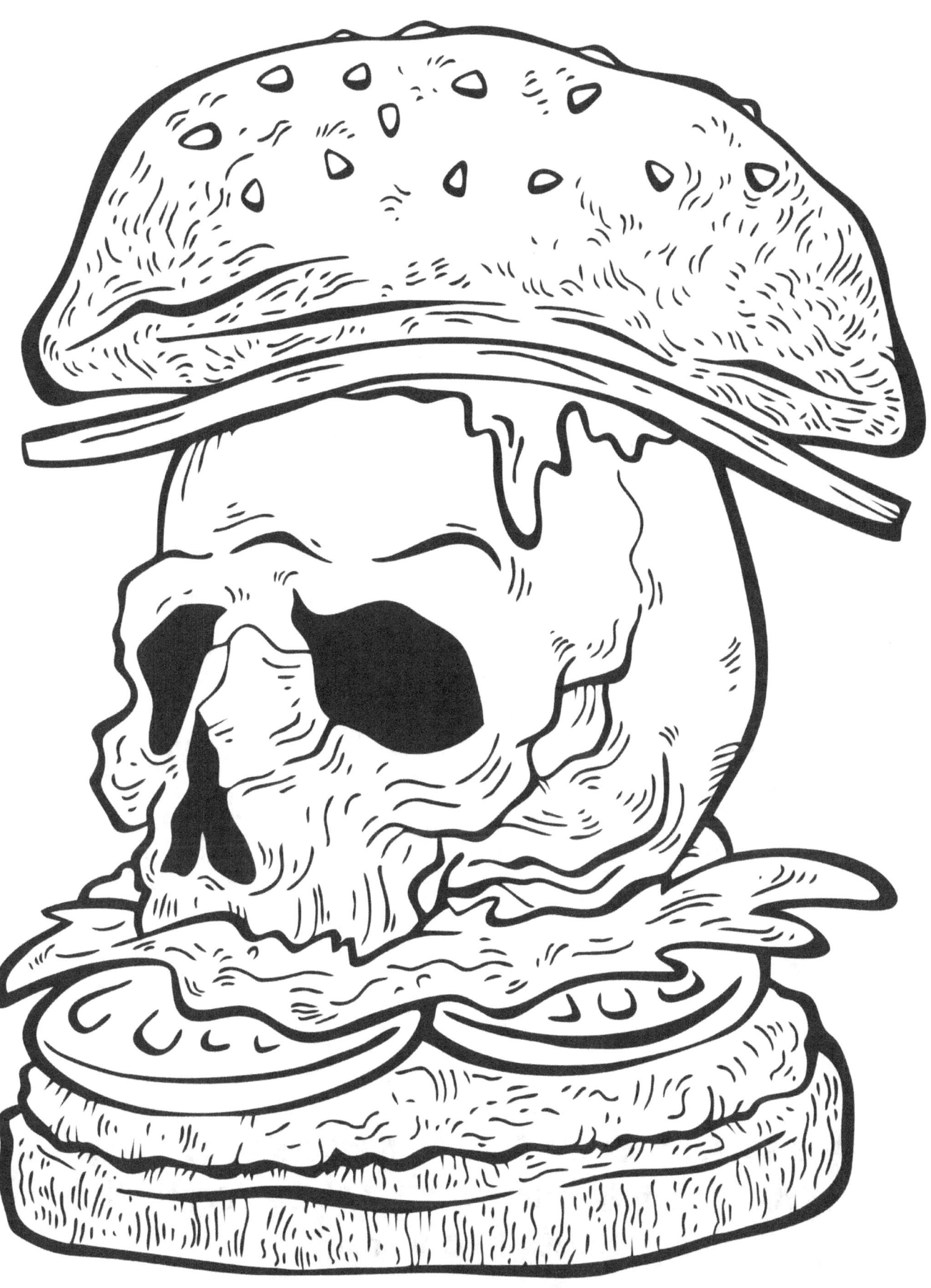

""Halloween wraps fear in innocence, as though it were a slightly sour sweet. Let terror, then, Be turned into a treat..."

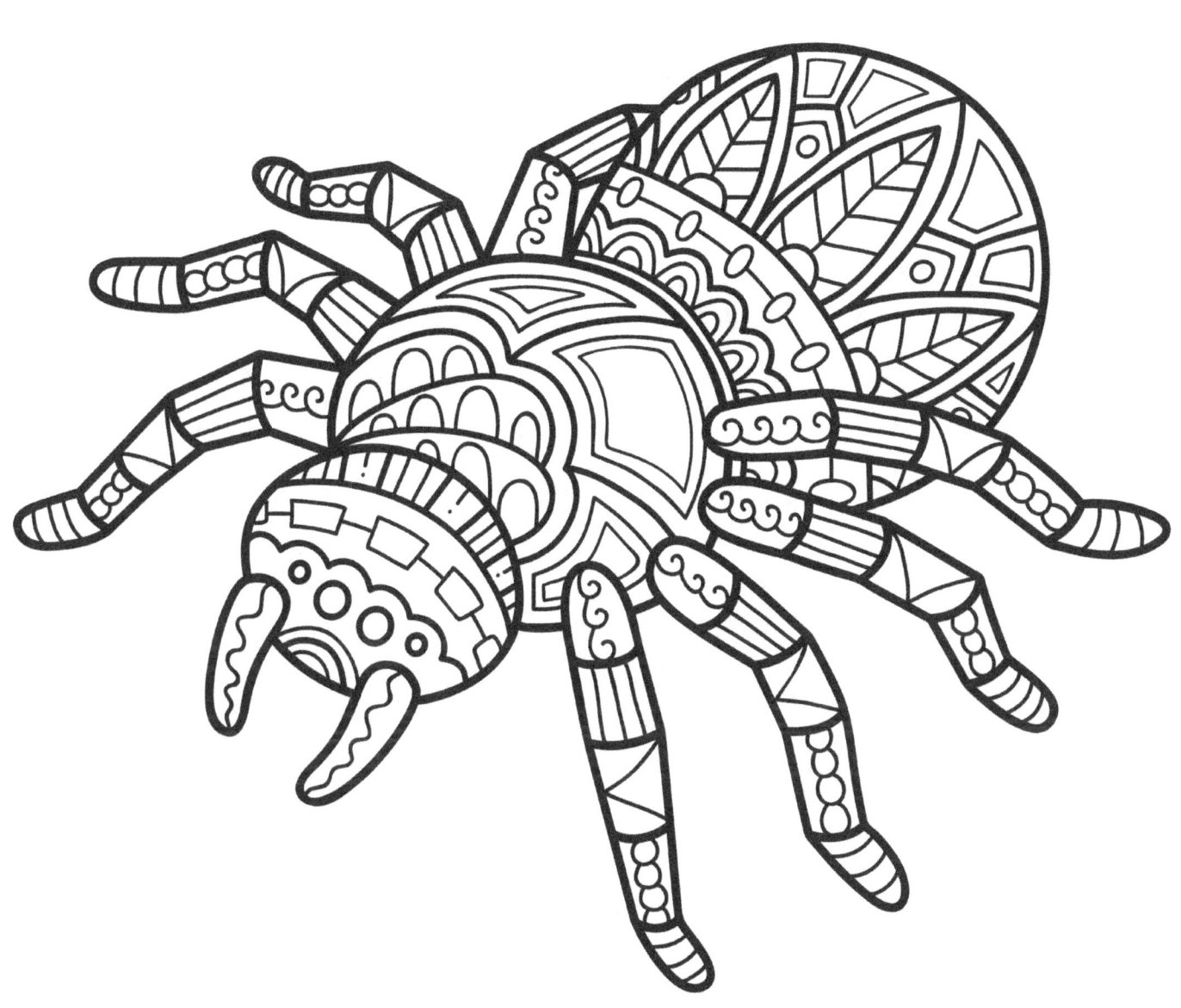

""Halloween wraps fear in innocence, as though it were a slightly sour sweet. Let terror, then, Be turned into a treat..."

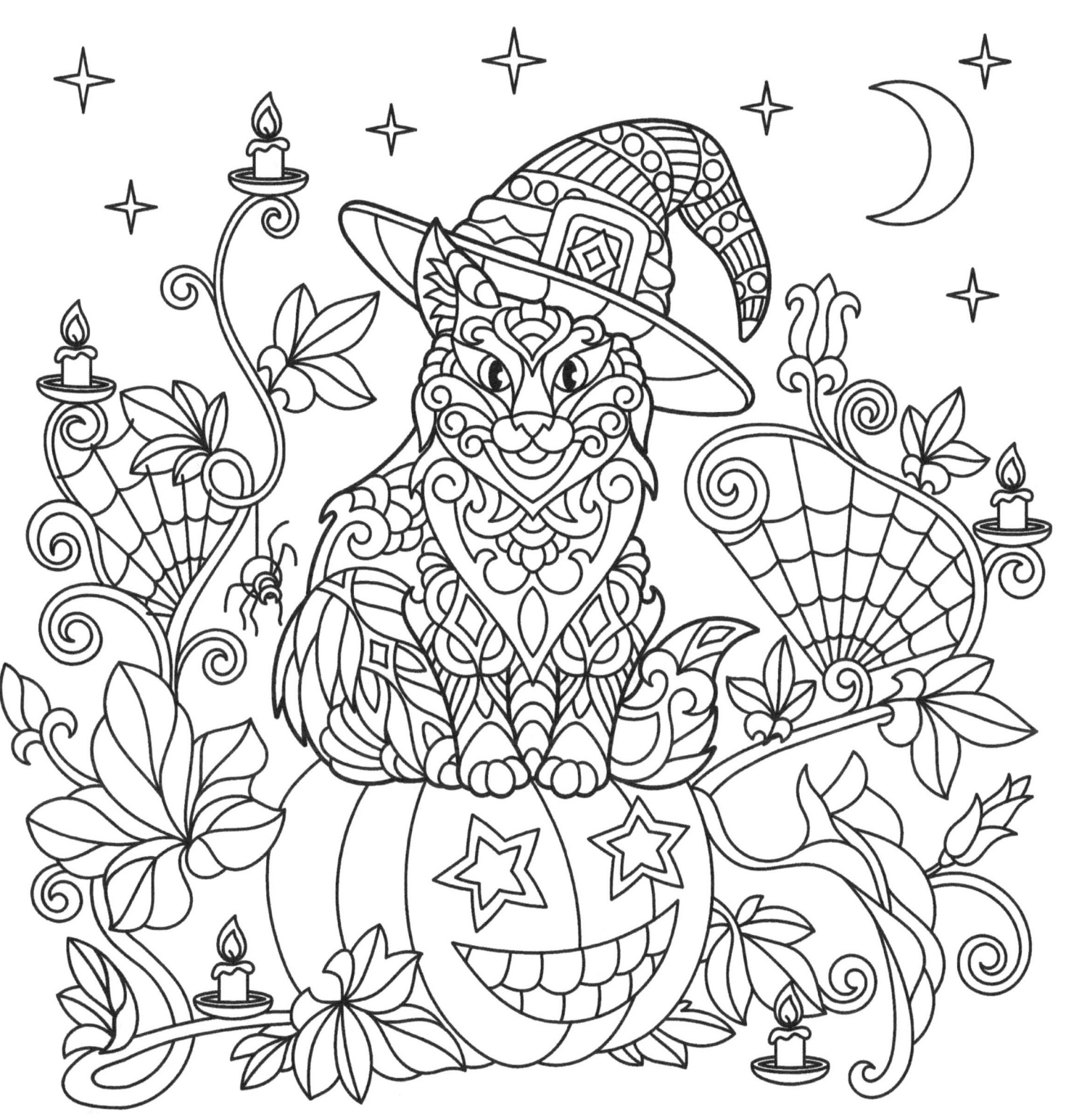